How Grand You Are

EDITED BY SARAH ARAK

Introduction

FOR MANY OF US, OUR FONDEST AND MOST CHERISHED FAMILY memories are those that involve our grandparents. Those lucky enough to know the unconditional love of a grandparent are forever touched by it; we carry it with us throughout our lives until we eventually become grandparents ourselves. When that happens, we understand, finally, what compels these lovely individuals to ask so little of their grandchildren, and to give them so much in return — pure, unadulterated love.

To a young grandchild, a grandparent is a treasure indeed, full of interesting bits of knowledge, fabulous stories, delicious recipes and giggly jokes. As we grow up, grandparents become bastions of wisdom to whom we turn when faced with important decisions. And what is a grandchild, to a grandparent? That's easy — a grandchild is the embodiment of perfection.

The bond between grandparents and grandchildren forges an indispensable connection that allows the wisdom and traditions of yesteryear to be carried forward into the future.

PERFECT LOVE SOMETIMES DOES NOT

COME UNTIL THE FIRST GRANDCHILD.

—Margaret Mead

My grandfather once told me that there are two kinds of people: those who work, and those who take the credit. He told me to try to be in the first group; there was less competition there.

—Indira Gandhi

WHAT CHILDREN NEED MOST ARE THE

ESSENTIALS THAT GRANDPARENTS PROVIDE:

UNCONDITIONAL LOVE, KINDNESS, PATIENCE,

HUMOR, COMFORT, LESSONS IN LIFE. AND,

MOST IMPORTANTLY, COOKIES.

—Rudolph Giuliani

FEW THINGS ARE MORE DELIGHTFUL

THAN GRANDCHILDREN FIGHTING

OVER YOUR LAP.

— Doug Larson

No COWBOY WAS EVER FASTER ON

THE DRAW THAN A GRANDPARENT PULLING

A BABY PICTURE OUT OF A WALLET.

—Author Unknown

M Y GRANDFATHER ALWAYS SAID THAT

LIVING IS LIKE LICKING HONEY OFF A THORN.

—Louis Adamic

A GRANDMOTHER IS A LITTLE BIT PARENT,

A LITTLE BIT TEACHER, AND

A LITTLE BIT BEST FRIEND.

—Author Unknown

WHO NEEDS SANTA...I GOT GRANDPA!

—Author Unknown

A CHILD NEEDS A GRANDPARENT,

ANYBODY'S GRANDPARENT,

TO GROW A LITTLE MORE SECURELY

INTO AN UNFAMILIAR WORLD.

— Charles and Ann Morse

A GRANDMOTHER PRETENDS SHE

DOESN'T KNOW WHO YOU ARE

ON HALLOWEEN.

—Erma Bombeck

THE REASON GRANDCHILDREN AND GRANDPARENTS

GET ALONG SO WELL IS THAT THEY

HAVE A COMMON ENEMY.

—Sam Levenson

WHAT IS IT ABOUT GRANDPARENTS THAT IS SO LOVELY?

I'D LIKE TO SAY THAT GRANDPARENTS ARE GOD'S

GIFTS TO CHILDREN. AND IF THEY CAN BUT SEE,

HEAR AND FEEL WHAT THESE PEOPLE HAVE

TO GIVE, THEY CAN MATURE AT A FASTER RATE.

—Bill Cosby

A GRANDMOTHER IS A BABYSITTER

WHO WATCHES THE KIDS INSTEAD

OF THE TELEVISION.

— Author Unknown

THEY SAY GENES SKIP GENERATIONS.

MAYBE THAT'S WHY GRANDPARENTS AND GRANDCHILDREN

FIND EACH OTHER SO LIKEABLE.

—Joan McIntosh

IT'S SUCH A GRAND THING TO BE A

MOTHER OF A MOTHER—THAT'S WHY THE

WORLD CALLS HER GRANDMOTHER.

—Author Unknown

GRANDCHILDREN DON'T STAY YOUNG

FOREVER, WHICH IS GOOD BECAUSE POP-POPS

HAVE ONLY SO MANY HORSEY RIDES IN THEM.

—Author Unknown

THE HISTORY OF OUR GRANDPARENTS IS REMEMBERED

NOT WITH ROSE PETALS BUT IN THE LAUGHTER AND

TEARS OF THEIR CHILDREN AND THEIR CHILDREN'S CHILDREN.

IT IS INTO US THAT THE LIVES OF GRANDPARENTS HAVE GONE.

IT IS IN US THAT THEIR HISTORY BECOMES A FUTURE.

—Charles and Ann Morse

NEVER HAVE CHILDREN, ONLY GRANDCHILDREN.

—Gore Vidal

GRANDMAS ARE MOMS WITH LOTS OF FROSTING!

—Author Unknown

BEING GRANDPARENTS SUFFICIENTLY

REMOVES US FROM THE RESPONSIBILITIES

SO THAT WE CAN BE FRIENDS.

—Allan Fromme

WE SHOULD ALL HAVE ONE PERSON WHO

KNOWS HOW TO BLESS US DESPITE THE EVIDENCE.

GRANDMOTHER WAS THAT PERSON TO ME.

—Phyllis Theroux

THERE'S NO PLACE LIKE HOME EXCEPT GRANDMA'S.

—Author Unknown

IF YOUR BABY IS BEAUTIFUL AND PERFECT,

NEVER CRIES OR FUSSES, SLEEPS ON SCHEDULE,

BURPS ON DEMAND AND IS AN ANGEL ALL THE TIME,

YOU'RE THE GRANDPARENT.

—Teresa Bloomingdale

BECOMING A GRANDMOTHER IS WONDERFUL.

ONE MOMENT YOU'RE JUST A MOTHER.

THE NEXT YOU ARE ALL-WISE AND PREHISTORIC.

—Pam Brown

WHAT A BARGAIN GRANDCHILDREN ARE!

I GIVE THEM MY LOOSE CHANGE, AND THEY GIVE

ME A MILLION DOLLARS WORTH OF PLEASURE.

—Gene Perret

My grandkids believe I'm the oldest thing in the world. And after two or three hours with them, I believe it, too.

—Author Unknown

THE SIMPLEST TOY, ONE WHICH EVEN THE

YOUNGEST CHILD CAN OPERATE,

IS CALLED A GRANDPARENT.

—Sam Levenson

JUST ABOUT THE TIME A WOMAN THINKS HER WORK

IS DONE, SHE BECOMES A GRANDMOTHER.

—Edward H. Dreschnack

GRANDCHILDREN ARE GOD'S WAY OF

COMPENSATING US FOR GROWING OLD.

—Mary H. Waldrip

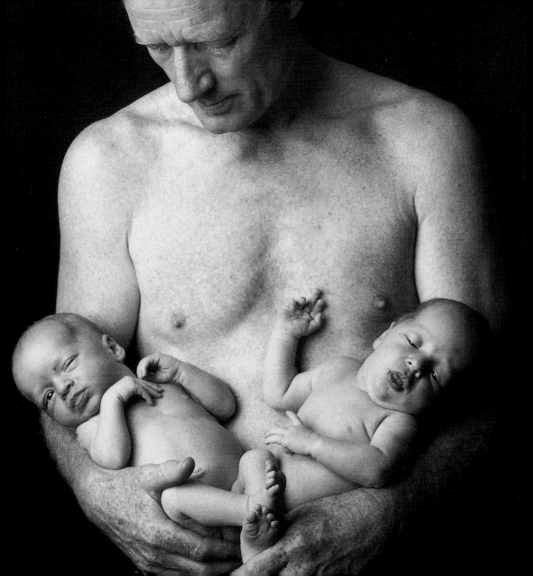

OUR GRANDCHILDREN ACCEPT US FOR OURSELVES,

WITHOUT REBUKE OR EFFORT TO CHANGE US, AS NO ONE

IN OUR ENTIRE LIVES HAS EVER DONE—NOT OUR PARENTS,

SIBLINGS, SPOUSES, FRIENDS, AND HARDLY EVER

OUR OWN GROWN CHILDREN.

—Ruth Goode

IF GOD HAD INTENDED US TO FOLLOW RECIPES,

HE WOULDN'T HAVE GIVEN US GRANDMOTHERS.

—Linda Henley

IF I HAD KNOWN HOW WONDERFUL

IT WOULD BE TO HAVE GRANDCHILDREN,

I'D HAVE HAD THEM FIRST.

—Lois Wyse

THE BEST BABY-SITTERS, OF COURSE, ARE THE

BABY'S GRANDPARENTS. YOU FEEL COMPLETELY

COMFORTABLE ENTRUSTING YOUR BABY TO THEM

FOR LONG PERIODS, WHICH IS WHY MOST

GRANDPARENTS FLEE TO FLORIDA.

—Dave Barry

GRANDMA ALWAYS MADE YOU FEEL SHE

HAD BEEN WAITING TO SEE YOU ALL DAY,

AND NOW THE DAY WAS COMPLETE.

—Marcy DeMaree

GRANDMAS HOLD OUR TINY HANDS

FOR JUST A LITTLE WHILE,

BUT OUR HEARTS FOREVER.

—Author Unknown

I HAVE A WARM FEELING AFTER

PLAYING WITH MY GRANDCHILDREN.

IT'S THE LINIMENT WORKING.

—Author Unknown

WHEN GRANDPARENTS ENTER THE DOOR,

DISCIPLINE FLIES OUT THE WINDOW.

—Ogden Nash

Nobody can do for little children

what grandparents do. Grandparents

sort of sprinkle stardust over the

lives of little children.

—Alex Haley

My GRANDFATHER WAS A WONDERFUL

ROLE MODEL. THROUGH HIM I GOT TO KNOW

THE GENTLE SIDE OF MEN.

—Sarah Long

ONE OF THE MOST POWERFUL HANDCLASPS

IS THAT OF A NEW GRANDBABY AROUND

THE FINGER OF A GRANDFATHER.

—Joy Hargrove

GRANDCHILDREN ARE THE GIFT

YOU GET FOR NOT STRANGLING

YOUR TEENAGERS.

—Author Unknown

THE BIRTH OF A GRANDCHILD IS A

WONDERFUL AND EXCITING EVENT THAT

CONTINUES THROUGHOUT LIFE.

—Tom Potts

PHOTO CREDITS